# A DAY IN THE LIFE

# Horses

### WHAT DO WILD HORSES LIKE MUSTANGS AND PONIES GET UP TO ALL DAY?

NEON SQUID

# Contents

2

# Welcome to the world of horses!

Wild horses are some of the most majestic and intriguing animals in the world! Their beauty captivated me when I was young, and I have spent my life surrounded by these amazing creatures. I am now a **biology professor** who studies animal behaviour. I've researched many different kinds of animals, but one of the first species I ever studied was horses. I've spent hours and hours watching their fascinating daily rituals, and I'm going to share what I have learned in this book!

Wild horses and their relatives are found all over the world. From zebras on the African savannah to the woolly horses of Mongolia, each species has its own set of **unique behaviours** and habits that helps it to survive in different circumstances.

There are so many amazing things to learn about our wild horses. How do they find food and water in the desert? What do they do when a new baby is born? How do they communicate with each other? I will explore these questions, and more, as we take a look at how wild horses spend a typical day!

**Dr Carly Anne York**

# Family tree

You can find horses and their relatives almost everywhere in the world. They belong to a larger group of animals called mammals. There are several different species of horse, all with their own distinguishing characteristics.

## Equidae

The family of horses and closely related animals, like donkeys and zebras, is called Equidae. This family also includes some extinct species known only from fossils dating back to 54 million years ago.

## Equus ferus caballus

This species includes all breeds of the domesticated horse (the horses humans ride), mustangs, and brumbies. Although mustangs and brumbies are often called "wild" horses, the correct term is "feral" – because they are descendants of domesticated horses.

"Domesticated" means tamed by humans.

## Equus ferus przewalskii

This species is known as the Przewalski's horse (pronounced "shuh-VAL-skee") and is the only truly wild horse that has not been domesticated. It is a rare species, and was once considered extinct in the wild. Through breeding efforts, it has been reintroduced to Mongolia.

## Equus asinus

This species includes domesticated and feral donkeys (or "burros"), as well as the wild asses of northern Africa. These animals resemble horses but have a large head, long ears, and a cow-like tail. They can be found anywhere in the world.

## Equus quagga

This species includes the plains zebra – the most common and widespread species of zebra in Africa. Its populations are decreasing because it is losing its habitat to farming. It is considered a threatened species.

# Brumbies on the move

In the hot, dry desert of Australia, the sun rises on the dark coat of an adult male brumby, a **stallion**. He walks behind a group of horses of all different colours – brown, grey, and even spotted. All the adult horses in this group are females, called **mares**, and the stallion is the father of the foals that walk by their side.

This group of horses have travelled together as a herd for years. The mares are loyal to the stallion, and in return he keeps them safe. He watches their surroundings with ears pricked up for any **possible threats**. Then he approaches a large grey female at the front of the herd, neighs softly to her, and they touch noses in a greeting. She is the lead mare of the group, and everyone will follow her guidance, including him. It hasn't rained in the desert for months, and the grasses are becoming shrivelled and dry. The herd is starting to get very thirsty. Their survival depends upon their ability to find water – and quickly!

The average lifespan of a wild horse is between 15 and 25 years.

# Roaming an abandoned city

As morning breaks, a group of Przewalski's horses roams through the abandoned city of Chernobyl in Ukraine, a country in Eastern Europe. This city is unoccupied by humans, but wildlife wanders in freely from the nearby forests.

In search of food, the curious herd enter a **deserted building**. They investigate their surroundings by sniffing with their noses in the air, but there's nothing tasty for them to eat here.

Horses can survive a few weeks without food, but only a few days without water.

These horses are unlike any others on Earth. They have small, brown, muscular bodies and tufted manes. Sadly, there are fewer than 2,000 Przewalski's horses left in the whole world! Because they're so rare, scientists call them an **endangered species**. They're working hard to ensure that these horses can thrive in the wild.

It's very cold, but the herd don't mind. They are used to frigid weather. The horses leave the city disappointed and hungry, as snow gently begins to fall.

# Clash of the mustangs

The morning sun shines on the plains of Nevada, USA. It's a peaceful scene, but it won't remain that way for much longer...

Mustangs live in groups made up of mares, their foals, and one **stallion**. A grey stallion has lived with this herd for years, and he has fought many times to maintain his position.

A brown stallion enters the scene. He is younger, and he's anxious to find a herd of his own. To do so, he must defeat the older stallion and steal his herd! The brown stallion charges at the grey stallion to try and scare him away, but instead he receives a swift and **dangerous kick** to the head. The two horses rear up on their hindlegs, thrashing at each other with their hooves. Neither horse holds back. After a few heavy blows, the brown stallion realises his opponent is too strong. He quickly retreats – the grey stallion is victorious!

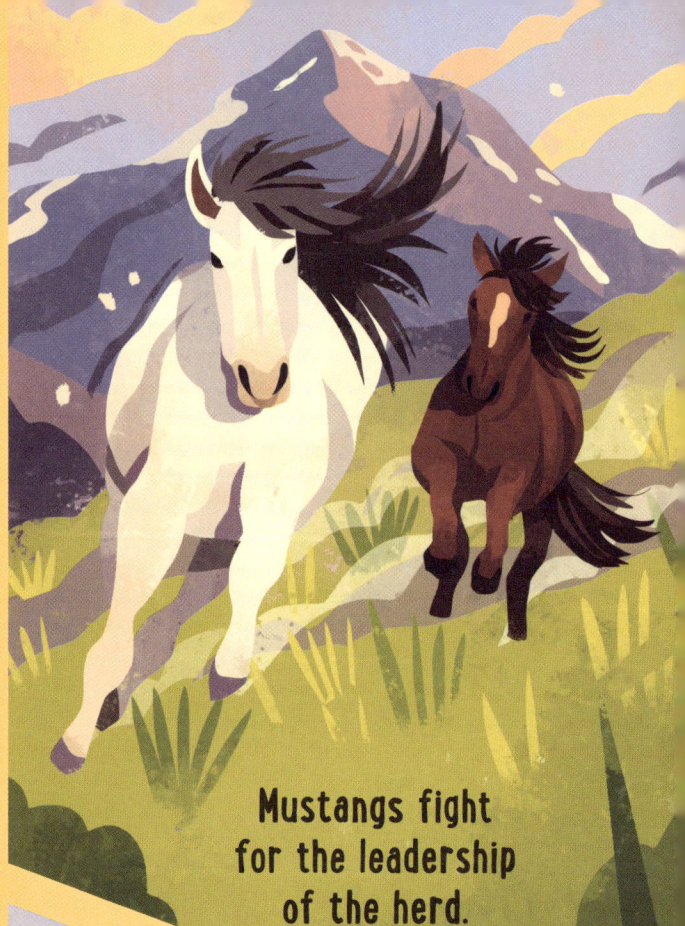

Mustangs fight for the leadership of the herd.

# A foal is born

In the lush countryside of England, a small, shaggy Dartmoor pony stands over her newborn foal. She carried her foal inside her for **11 months**, and she is very excited to meet the little creature at her feet.

Softly, she nuzzles the new baby as he opens his eyes for the very first time. She licks his soft, downy coat and encourages him to stand. Unlike many other baby animals, horses can **stand up** within hours of being born!

The foal stretches out his gangly legs and jumps up in a wobble. He takes his first shaky steps and clumsily falls to his knees – but quickly he regains his balance. He staggers over to his mother and licks at her coat. Before long, he finds the comfort of her **warm milk**, and nurses contentedly by her side.

A foal will drink its mother's milk for four to six months before it starts to eat grass.

# Colours and patterns

The modern horse has many different coat colours, ranging from white to black. Some colours have been bred for many generations, but what did the wild horses that lived thousands of years ago look like? Scientists have used samples from fossils to confirm that horses had five main colours – including the spotted pattern still seen in horses today!

### Leopard-spotted

Leopard-spotted horses had white coats with black or brown spots. Their manes and tails could be dark- or light-coloured.

### Black

Black horses had dark skin with very dark brown or black coats. Their manes and tails were also black.

### Bay

Bay horses had brown coats ranging from dark to light shades. Their legs, manes, and tails were black.

## Cave paintings

About 25,000 years ago, humans began painting horses on the walls of caves with charcoal and dirt. Scientists have found more than 100 painted caves that show over 4,000 different kinds of animals!

## Grulla

Grulla horses had grey hairs on their bodies, with a dark strip running down their backs. Their legs, manes, and tails were black.

## Dun

Dun horses had tan hairs on their bodies with a dark strip running down their backs. Their legs, manes, and tails were black.

# Splashing in the surf

In the south of France, a herd of **white horses** gallops through the marshes that border the Mediterranean Sea. They are small horses, with strong legs and tough hooves to help them move through the marshes. They are also considered to be especially intelligent.

The Camargue horses have lived in these wetlands for **thousands of years**. They are thought to be one of the oldest living breeds of horse in the world! Although it is clear they have lived here for a long time, no one is sure where they first came from.

Long manes and tails protect the Camargue horses from pesky insects.

The horses navigate their swampy home as a herd, with the lead mare guiding the way. They nibble on the tough, salty grasses that grow around the marshland, and they splash in the waters. The horses aren't the only animals to enjoy this beautiful place. Above, a group of **pink flamingos** fly past!

**Meanwhile...** As the brumbies search for water, one of the foals gets tired and falls behind the herd. Her mother whinnies to her, encouraging her to keep up.

# A storm on the horizon

The Dartmoor ponies are grazing on lush, green grass high up in the hills. The ponies are **small and sturdy** and come in a range of different colours. Their thick, shaggy hair keeps them warm in all sorts of conditions.

Protected in the middle of the herd are the mother and her new foal. Only two hours have passed, but already he is walking strongly with the herd. His ability to walk so steadily allows him to stay safe from **potential predators**. For the next year, he'll be safe by his mother's side – resting, nursing, and absorbing his new world.

The wind is beginning to blow and storm clouds are gathering overhead. The ponies lift their heads as the sky starts to darken. They can smell that **rain is on the way**.

**Meanwhile...** Smarting from his loss to the grey stallion, the brown mustang retreats to a group of young males. Together they form what is known as a bachelor herd.

# Beware the coyote

In the desert of Arizona, USA, a burro – a **wild donkey** – walks by himself through the dry, hot terrain. Unlike horses, burros don't always travel in herds, and the males stake out territories.

In the distance is the faintest rustle. The burro stops and turns his full attention to the sound.

His large ears prick forward with attention and his nostrils flare as he picks up a scent – a predator is nearby!

A coyote quietly crawls out of the brush and into view. The burro stands his ground. And then, without hesitation, he charges! Teeth bared and ears flattened, he **runs at full speed** towards the coyote. The wild dog sprints back into the brush of the desert. Proud of his success, the burro continues on his way, munching on the dry, rough grass as he goes.

# At the watering hole

It's a hot afternoon in the South African savannah, as a herd of zebras approaches a watering hole. They lower their heads to take a crisp, cool drink. Their **black and white stripes** create a dizzying sight – it's hard to tell where one zebra begins and the other one ends! Their dazzling patterns might keep them safe by confusing nearby predators.

Similarly to the brumbies, zebra herds have one stallion and multiple females that travel in a group. Watering holes are scarce in this part of the world, and the zebras aren't the only ones who are thirsty. They are joined by all kinds of other wildlife: giraffes, elephants, water buffalo – even lions!

The zebras slowly walk a little deeper into the water, cooling their hot bodies, but they need to be careful: **crocodiles** are known to swim in these waters too...

Zebras recognise each other by their unique patterns of stripes.

### Eohippus

Eohippus appeared about 52 million years ago and was approximately the size of a fox. Its front legs had four toes, while its back legs had three toes – each with small hooves!

### Mesohippus

Mesohippus appeared about 40 million years ago and was larger with longer legs. It walked on three toes with hooves, but the middle one was stronger than the outer ones.

### Merychippus

Merychippus appeared about 15 million years ago and looked a bit like a small pony. It also had three toes, but it only walked on the middle one, which had a hoof.

# The evolution of horses

Wild horses are well adapted to the harsh environments where they live, thanks to about 60 million years of evolution. Throughout this time they have very slowly changed from small animals, no larger than dogs, to the amazing animals that roam the world today.

## Pliohippus

Pliohippus appeared about 12 million years ago and looked like a modern horse. It walked on one toe with a hoof, and the other two toes were barely visible stubs.

## Equus

Equus, the modern horse, appeared about four million years ago. It is larger and has longer legs than its ancestors. Equus is the last common ancestor of Przewalski's horses, burros, and zebras.

## Meet the family

Although they don't look like family, the closest relatives to the horse are the tapir and the rhinoceros! These animals are grouped with horses because they all have an odd number of toes.

# Searching in the snow

It is late afternoon, and the snow has continued to fall all day. The Przewalski's horses have not had any luck finding food, and they are becoming tired and hungry. They **paw at the icy ground** in the hope of uncovering a patch of green grass, but all they find is dirt.

A blanket of snow sits on the horses' backs, but their thick winter coats protect them from the cold. Their hair stands upright, giving them a fluffy appearance and trapping warm air next to their skin. Natural oils in their coats also help repel water as if they are wearing **raincoats**. The horses began growing their winter coats months ago – surprisingly, it is the dark, short days that stimulate coat growth and not the cooler temperatures!

Millions of years of evolution have prepared the Przewalski's horses for treacherous snowstorms just like this one, and they continue undeterred in their search for something to eat.

# Digging a well

Thirsty from his earlier clash with the coyote, the burro has an idea. He begins digging in the desert sand... He paws at the ground, throwing the sand behind him like a dog burying a bone.

He digs and digs until he is standing in a knee-deep hole, when suddenly water appears! He has successfully dug a **drinking well**, and he excitedly slurps up the water to quench his thirst. The clever burro drinks his fill and continues on his way, leaving the well behind.

30

The fennec fox, the smallest fox species, enjoys a drink from the well.

But water never goes to waste in a desert! Other animals follow the burro's lead, sipping from this water hole. Wells like this often become growing sites for plants as well. The burro has done a great service to the whole **ecosystem** by providing a source of water for plants and animals alike!

Prairie dogs live in tight family groups. They all appreciate a sip of water!

# The brown foal

The Camargue horses are gathered together after their romp through the wetlands. They quietly graze on tall grasses and explore the marshy shoreline. A few are resting, which horses can do either **standing up** or lying down!

In the group of white horses, there is one mysterious outlier – a brown foal nursing by her mother's side. Why is this foal brown, when both her mother and father are white?

Well, all of the white horses were born brown too! Even horses that appear to be white have **dark skin** underneath their coats of hair. The Camargue horses become lighter and lighter as they get older, until all of their brown baby hair has turned to silver. This little foal is no exception, and in a few years she will look just like the rest of the herd!

**Meanwhile...** The storm has caught up with the Dartmoor ponies. They stand together with their backs to the wind and their heads held low. Their coats keep their skin dry in even the worst rainstorms.

# Fly swatters

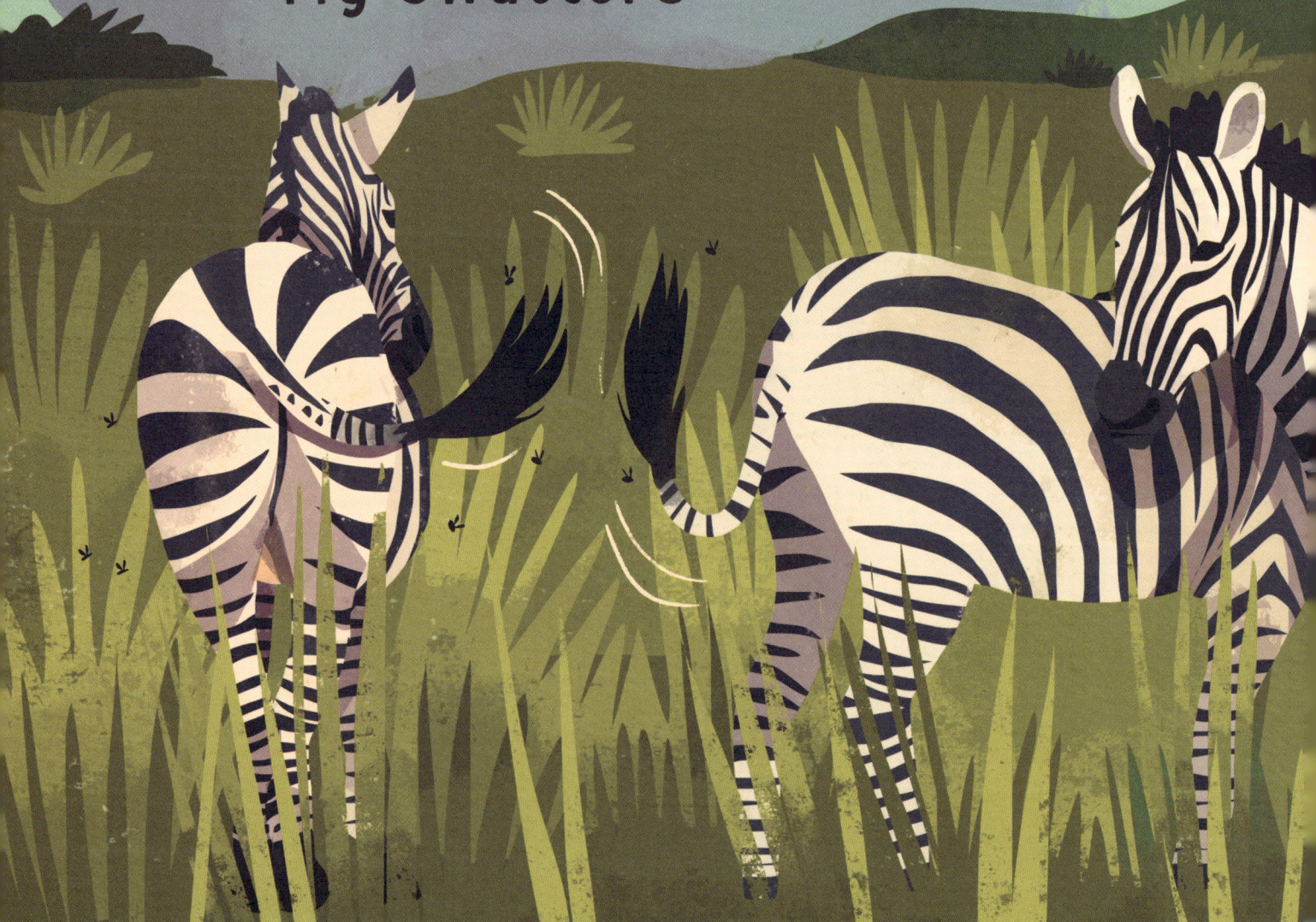

In the grassy savannah, the zebra herd is resting and grazing in the early evening light. A few zebras have paired off, standing head to tail. Their wispy tails **flick away flies** from their partners' faces while they gently nibble on each other's shoulders. Not only does this activity feel good, but it also helps the zebras bond with each other.

Compared to the antelope grazing nearby, the zebras have barely any flies on them at all. Why could this be?

Surprisingly, scientists have found that the **striped pattern** of the zebras' coats actually helps to repel flies! When flies get near to a zebra, they can get confused by its stripes. As a result, they don't know where to land! Time to find an antelope instead...

# Communication

Horses have two ways in which they can communicate – by using their voices and through body language. When a horse uses its voice, it can be a soft neigh or a loud, urgent whinny. Body language ranges from a subtle shift of the ears to a dangerous kick. Both forms of communicating are important for these social animals.

## Ears

Horses can move their ears in different directions to indicate how they are feeling. Ears that are pricked forwards show alertness or happiness. Ears that are pinned back show aggression. Horses can also move their ears to listen.

**Horses use muscles in their faces to pull a variety of expressions.**

## Legs

Using their legs is the most dangerous way in which horses communicate. They can rear up and thrash at the air to challenge another horse, or they can deliver a deadly kick with their hindlegs.

## Neck

Horses will arch their necks to make themselves look bigger and more dominant. If they want to look smaller and more submissive to another horse, they will lower their heads and necks.

## Mouth

Horses will roll their upper lips into the air when they are smelling another horse. They can also use their mouths to groom each other gently, or to bite in an aggressive encounter!

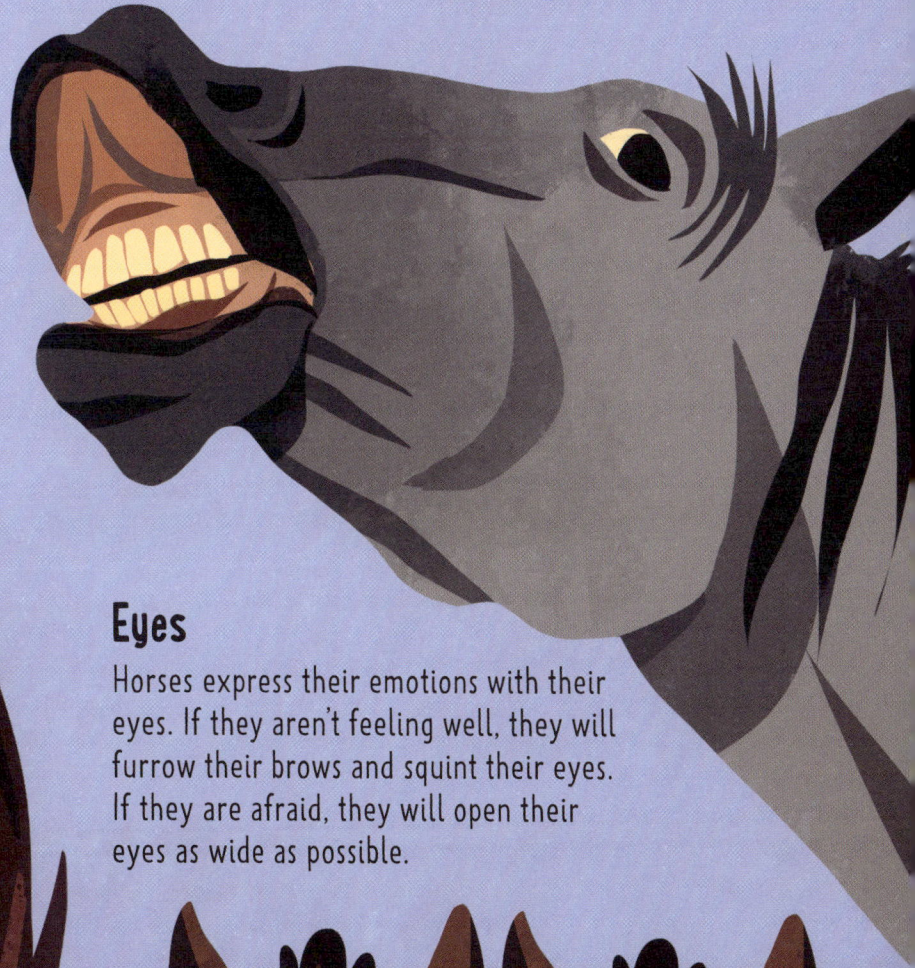

## Tail

A quick swish of a horse's tail lets you know it is annoyed. A tail lifted high in the air shows excitement!

## Eyes

Horses express their emotions with their eyes. If they aren't feeling well, they will furrow their brows and squint their eyes. If they are afraid, they will open their eyes as wide as possible.

# The search continues

The brumbies have been desperately searching for water for half a day now. The lead mare has guided the herd to every watering hole she knows, but it has been so hot that the water has evaporated. The herd trudges through the **Australian outback**, moving slowly to save energy.

The dark stallion walks behind the herd, constantly on the watch for predators. The foals are becoming weaker, and the sun is setting. Soon **coyotes and wild dogs** will be on the hunt, and the stallion must stay alert.

But what is that in the distance? Just in time, a watering hole is in sight! The brumbies pick up the pace. Eventually they make it to the edge of the watering hole and joyfully plunge their noses into the water. Their search is over!

# Dinner is served

The Przewalski's horses have been searching for food all day, but their hopes of finding anything to eat before dark are **growing slim**. The horses huddle together with their backs to the wind, trying to stay warm as the snow continues to fall. Some of them lie down to rest after the long, weary day.

But there's a noise in the distance that catches their attention and a smell that lifts their spirits – hay! Scientists have been keeping a close eye on the Przewalski's horses. Although they want the horses to find their own food, the scientists also want to ensure that this **endangered species** is safe. The horses excitedly gather around the hay bales and munch happily into the night.

**Meanwhile...** Scorching desert temperatures during the day mean that the burro waits until night-time to search for food. This helps him to stay cool and hydrated.

Hay is dried grass
that can be stored for
feeding horses.

In the darkness, the zebra herd gathers together for a peaceful evening. The mares lie down to rest their tired bodies, but the stallion stands on watch nearby. He is the guardian of the herd and has to remain alert at all times – listening and looking out for nearby threats. Zebras have many **predators**, including lions, cheetahs, and hyenas, so they must always be aware of their surroundings...

Suddenly the stallion hears something – a rustling in the brush! In the distance, the eyes of a **pack of hyenas** glow. The hyenas are watching the zebra herd and waiting for a moment to strike. They try to be quiet, but zebras have exceptional hearing. As soon as the stallion hears the rustling, he loudly brays to the herd. They jump to their feet and gallop away into the night! The hyenas are left confused and hungry. They will need to find a different meal tonight.

## Zebras will circle a wounded herd member to protect them from a predator.

# The end of a long day

The grey mustang stallion stands under a starry sky. He narrowly escaped losing his herd today, and he has the **battle wounds** to show for it. The kick marks from the dark stallion have begun to swell, and his coat shows the marks of teeth.

Despite his injuries, he is happy to have won the fight with the bachelor stallion. He stands by his herd of mares, who have lain down to sleep for the evening.

The stallion is tired too, but he needs to stay awake to listen for predators such as mountain lions and wolves.

Luckily it is a peaceful evening, and the only sounds are the wind rustling through the shrubby trees and an **owl hooting** from above. The crickets are chirping a joyful lullaby in the distance. The stallion enjoys the calm, and closes his eyes to rest.

# Glossary

**Ass**
An animal in the horse family that is smaller than a horse and has long ears, a cow-like tail, and a braying call. Ass is another name for a donkey.

**Bachelor herd**
A herd of young male horses who have not formed their own herd of mares yet.

**Brumby**
A type of feral horse found in Australia.

**Burro**
An animal in the horse family that is smaller than a horse and has long ears, a cow-like tail, and a braying call. Burro is the Spanish word for "donkey".

**Domesticated**
Tamed and bred by humans to be kept as a pet or work animal.

**Ecosystem**
Animals and plants interacting together in their environment.

**Endangered**
At risk of extinction.

**Equidae**
The family of horses and related animals, including donkeys, zebras, and extinct species.

**Evolution**
The process by which species change over time.

**Extinct**
When no members of a particular species are alive today.

**Feral**
An animal in the wild that has escaped from captivity, or has descended from animals that escaped from captivity.

**Foal**
A young horse.

**Habitat**
The natural home of an animal.

**Mammal**
An animal that has hair or fur, and the females of the species produce milk for their offspring.

**Mane**
Growth of long hair on the neck of a horse.

**Mare**
A female horse.

**Mustang**
A type of feral horse found in the USA.

**Predator**
An animal that eats other animals.

**Stallion**
A male horse.

## Energy

Machines make electricity using the energy of ocean water and winds. Oil and natural gas, which are burned to make heat, are pumped from beneath the ocean floor.

## Transport

Boats carry people and products, from cars to coal, from island to island or from port to port.

Arctic Ocean

Indian Ocean

## Resources

The ocean offers us resources, which are materials that we can use, from beautiful pearls to tasty salt.

# Trawling the Oceans

**Across the world's oceans, people work on fishing boats large and small.**

**They hope to catch fish to sell or to feed their families.**

It is very hard work on a fishing boat. During storms, the boat is battered by high waves and strong winds.

When it is hot, workers sweat beneath the burning Sun. In cold weather, they are soaked by the chilly waves, so they must wear warm, waterproof clothes.

Trawlers are boats that drag fishing nets through the water behind them. The nets fill up with fish. Sometimes dolphins or sharks are trapped accidentally, so when workers haul the nets on board, they must take care to free them. Workers must also be careful not to catch too many of one fish species. This is called overfishing. When a species is overfished, there are not enough adult fish to make babies. This puts the species at risk of extinction.

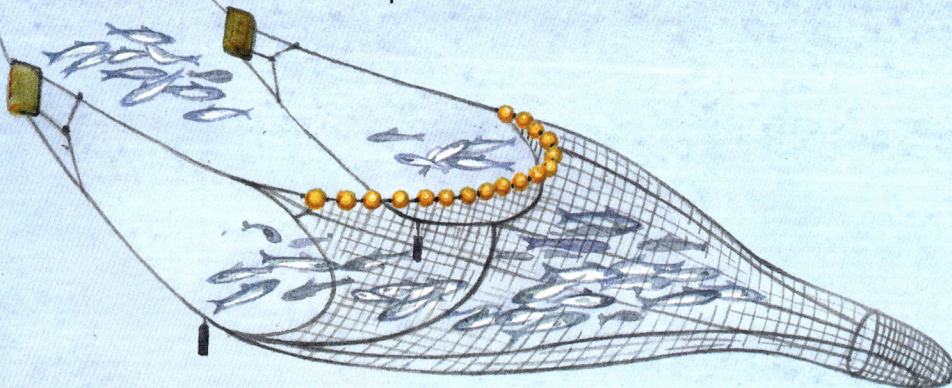

# Fishing by the Coast

**Along the coast, the shallow water is busy with fish and other creatures.**

**People use traps and tricks to catch them for their dinner, for supermarkets or for restaurants.**

Fish can be caught using hand-held nets, spears or fishing rods. At the end of a fishing rod is a line attached to a hook. Bait is put on the hook so fish will bite it. The bait may be a wriggling maggot or a bright feather that looks like an insect. In the Indian Ocean, Sri Lankan fishermen perch on poles so they can see fish in the shallow water, but the fish cannot see them.

Sometimes, coastal sea creatures are caught in traps built from nets, stones or narrowly spaced wooden poles. Lobsters are caught in traps made of wood, wire or net. They crawl in through a small opening, but cannot find their way out.

# Index

## This has been a

# NEON ![squid logo] SQUID

## production

*This book is dedicated to my parents, who raised me on books like this one. They nurtured my obsession with horses and supported me on my path to becoming a biologist. I'd also like to express deep appreciation to my husband, who knew I would be a scientist long before I knew it myself.*

**Author:** Dr Carly Anne York
**Illustrator:** Chaaya Prabhat

### Neon Squid would like to thank:

Allison Singer-Kushnir for editing the American edition, and Georgina Coles for proofreading.

Copyright © 2022 St. Martin's Press
120 Broadway, New York, NY 10271

Created for St. Martin's Press
by Neon Squid
The Stables, 4 Crinan Street,
London, N1 9XW

EU representative: Macmillan
Publishers Ireland Ltd,
1st Floor, The Liffey Trust Centre,
117–126 Sheriff Street Upper,
Dublin 1, D01 YC43

10 9 8 7 6 5 4 3 2 1

The right of Dr Carly Anne York to be identified as the author of this work has been asserted in accordance with the Copyright, Designs and Patents Act, 1988.

A CIP catalogue record for this book is available from the British Library.

Printed and bound by Vivar Printing in Malaysia.

ISBN: 978-1-83899-230-9

www.neonsquidbooks.com

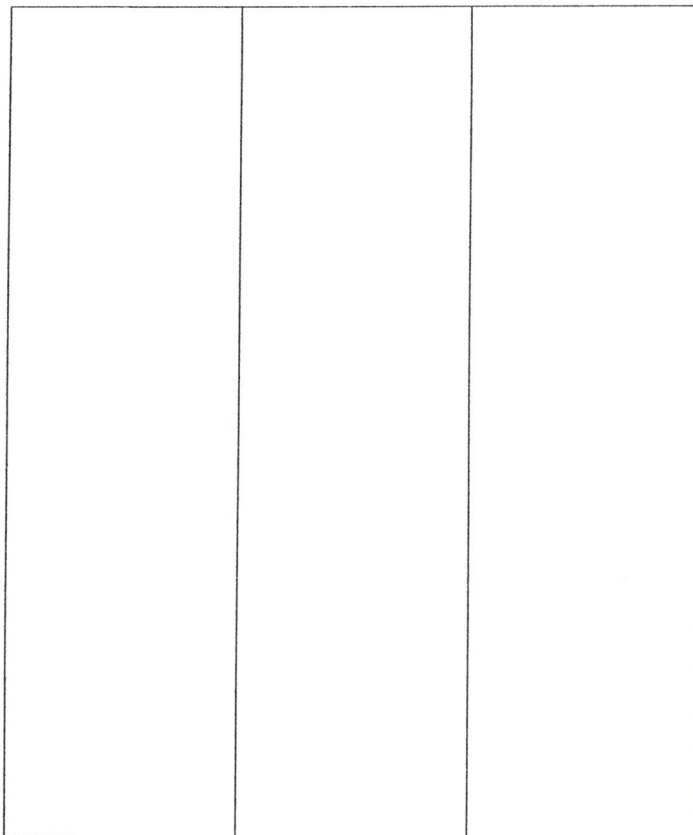

This book is on loan from Library Services for Schools